1 MONTH OF
FREE
READING

at

www.ForgottenBooks.com

By purchasing this book you are eligible for one month membership to ForgottenBooks.com, giving you unlimited access to our entire collection of over 1,000,000 titles via our web site and mobile apps.

To claim your free month visit:

www.forgottenbooks.com/free71735

ISBN 978-0-484-57959-9
PIBN 10071735

This book is a reproduction of an important historical work. Forgotten Books uses
state-of-the-art technology to digitally reconstruct the work, preserving the original format
whilst repairing imperfections present in the aged copy. In rare cases, an imperfection in
the original, such as a blemish or missing page, may be replicated in our edition. We do,
however, repair the vast majority of imperfections successfully; any imperfections that
remain are intentionally left to preserve the state of such historical works.

Politics and Religion.

❧❧❧

BEFORE the Presidential Election of November, 1908, in the United States, President Roosevelt received several letters in which the fear was expressed that the best interests of the country might be endangered by the election to the presidential office of the Honorable William H. Taft, the Republican candidate, because of his Unitarian belief, but especially because of his reputed sympathy with the Roman Catholic Church.

Immediately after the election, under date of 6 November, 1908, President Roosevelt addressed a public letter [1] to Mr. J. C. Martin, Dayton, Ohio, which, in purpose and effect, was an answer to all who had written to him on the subject of religion in politics. The secular press of the country was practically unanimous in its approbation of the President's attitude, and unquestionably gave expression to the enlightened and best opinion of the general body of the American people.

The note of dissent was soon sounded by certain sectarian bodies, notably the Lutherans and Baptists. The New York City Synodical Conference of the Evangelical Lutheran Church of

[1] Given in the Appendix, pp. 59-63.

3

America, in an open letter [2] to the President, 14 November, 1908, quoted from the Bulls issued by Boniface VIII, Pius IX, and Leo XIII, and asked " are we not then compelled to maintain that a loyal Roman Catholic who fully understands the allegiance required of him by the Pope can never sincerely subscribe to the Federal Constitution, nor, if he does subscribe to it, never can be expected to abide by it, enforce, and defend it?"

Three days later, the Lutheran Pastoral Association and the German Lutheran Pastoral Conference, at a meeting held in Philadelphia, 16 November, 1908, reiterated the sentiments of their brethren in New York and embodied their protest also in a letter [3] to the President.

Before the end of the same month the Philadelphia Conference of Baptist Ministers discussed at length the President's letter, and finally deemed it wise and fitting to adopt a series of resolutions,[4] in which they impugn the civil allegiance of the Catholics of the United States, and urge them " to assert their right to think and act in harmony with the governmental ideas of their own country."

In view of this demand of the Baptists upon the laymen of the Catholic Church, and, especially because of the specific charges of disloyalty

[2] Appendix, pp. 63-66.

[3] Appendix, pp. 67-71.

[4] Appendix, pp. 71-73.

against Catholics on the part of the Lutherans, the following speech of the Honorable Joseph R. Chandler,[5] Member of Congress from Pennsylvania, delivered in the Second Session of the Thirty-third Congress, 10 January, 1855, has a special and timely interest.

The judicious and dispassionate reading of Mr. Chandler's memorable speech will unfold the views which a Catholic layman, a scholar, a litterateur, a statesman and one of Philadelphia's first citizens a half-century ago, boldly and eloquently expressed in the legislative halls at Washington, in refutation of the base and oft-repeated charge that a Roman Catholic could not be a loyal American citizen.

The very substance of the calumny so deliberately put forth afresh by the Lutheran and Baptist Ministers is found in the attack of the Honorable Nathaniel Banks. It should be said, however, that Mr. Banks was a layman and, likely, ill-informed of the history of the Catholic Church and incapable of understanding the true and full meaning of her doctrines. This extenuating circumstance is not found in the bigoted utterances made by ministers of the Gospel, some of them professors in theological seminaries, and capable, or at least reputed to be so, of reading aright the history of the Church and understanding the nature and significance of ecclesiastical documents and decrees.

[5] A brief sketch of Mr. Chandler's career is given in the Appendix, pp. 57-58.

That the Catholic layman of the present generation is no less zealous and able to defend the Church, and no less ready to make public profession of his faith than the layman of fifty years ago, is evidenced by the splendid oration of the Honorable Bourke Cochran, of New York, at the Catholic Missionary Congress held in Chicago, 18 November, 1908. His eloquent exposition of the Catholic Church's teaching regarding the duty of civil allegiance of her members was elicited by the Lutheran Ministers' attack on the patriotism of Catholics. In this it is the same to-day as it was fifty years ago, the attack comes from the Protestant camp. Mr. Chandler did not seek the controversy. At the conclusion of his speech he tells us this: " Mr. Chairman," he says, " I have forborne to-day all retaliatory imputations, all irritating comparisons, and confined myself to a refutation of a charge made against men of the Roman Catholic Creed. I have not sought this contest, but, for the sake of honor, of truth, of myself and my co-religionists, for the sake of the institutions and the Constitution of my Country, I could not decline it. I have evaded no point, nor attempted to darken counsel. I have met the charge fairly, candidly, and truthfully."

Temporal Power of the Pope.*

❦❦❦

Speech of Hon. J. R. Chandler,

of Pennsylvania,

In the House of Representatives,

10 January, 1855.

THE House being in Committee of the Whole on the state of the Union—

MR. CHANDLER said: I rise to express my opinions on a subject which ought never to have been introduced into the Congress of the United States; but, having been brought hither and discussed, the suggestions of many friends lead me to believe that it is my duty to present, not merely my opinions, but certain facts in relation thereto.

I purpose making some reply to the remarks of the honorable gentleman from Massachusetts (Mr. Banks), who recently addressed this House, in committee, on some of the prevailing topics of the day, and made special and inculpatory allusion to the creed of the Roman Catholic

---

¹ The foot-notes throughout this memorable speech have been added by the present editor, who has had all quotations carefully verified and supplied the references to their exact sources.

Church; involving a charge of latent treason against its members, or at least imputing to them an article of religious faith that overrides all fealty to the Government of the country, and would render them unworthy of public trust— suspected citizens, and dangerous officers.

Before I commence my direct reference to the subject of my remarks, let me say that, whatever may be my religious belief and connexions, I trust that all who know me in this House will acquit me of the charge of any attempt to obtrude those opinions upon others, or to press upon my associates, publicly or privately, any defense of the creed of my Church, or the peculiarity of its forms and ceremonies. Believing, sir, that religion is a personal matter, I have avoided public exhibition of my pretensions; and, knowing the unpopularity of my creed, I have been careful not to jeopard my means of usefulness, in their legitimate channel, by any untimely presentation of irrelevant and unacceptable dogmas.

But now, sir, I think I cannot be deceived in supposing that a well-tempered reply would not only be patiently received in this House, but that an attempt at such a reply as the charge of the gentleman from Massachusetts would suggest to a Catholic, is expected from me, as the oldest of the few, the very few, (I know but one besides myself in this House), who are obnoxious to any censures justly made against professors of the Catholic religion, and who may be directly interested in a defense from imputations of a want of fealty to the Government of the country, in consequence of the nature of their obligations to the Catholic Church.

If, Mr. Chairman, I had not long been a member of this House, and thus become able to form an opinion of the honorable gentlemen who compose it, I might startle at the risk of presenting myself as the professor of a creed " everywhere evil spoken of," and standing almost alone in the assertion of a fact which seems to be everywhere doubted. I stand, too, sir, without the sympathies of a host of partisans to sustain me in my weakness, and to pardon me in the infirmities of my defense in consequence of their attachment to the principles I advocate.

I stand alone, indeed; the generous defense offered by the gentleman from South Carolina (Mr. Keitt), and the gentleman from Mississippi (Mr. Barry), was the magnaminous effort of men who would defend the *professors* of a creed which they do not hold. I, sir, speak for a creed which I do hold. I stand alone, sir; but I stand in the Congress of the nation. I stand among gentlemen. I stand for truth; and how feeble soever may be my effort, I feel that I may continue to depend, at least, upon the forbearance of a body that has always entitled itself to my gratitude by its unfailing courtesy to my humble exertions.

Mr. Chairman, I understand the honorable gentleman from Massachusetts (Mr. Banks), in his defense of the secret combination to put down the Catholic religion in this country, by denying to its members the full rights of citizenship, to assert that he does not bring into discussion the general creed of the Catholics, but only that portion which, it is asserted, makes the professor dependent upon the Bishop of Rome, not merely for what he shall hold of faith toward God, but what he shall maintain of fealty toward his own political Government.

Let me read a paragraph from the published remarks of the honorable gentleman:

MR. BANKS.—I have no objection to any man of the Catholic Church, or faith. Here is our friend from Pennsylvania (Mr. Chandler), an amiable, learned, and eloquent man; I might be willing to vote for him, Catholic as he is, in preference, perhaps to others nearer my political faith than he is. What he thinks of the Seven Sacraments, or how many he accepts is no concern of mine. To me it is no objection that he receives the interpretations of the Council of Trent as to the doctrines of original sin and justification. It cannot concern me, and it can concern no man, that, as a matter of faith, any person cherishes the doctrine of transubstantiation, accords the full measure of Catholic veneration to sacred relics or images, and accepts every article of the Nicene Creed. Each man is accountable for his own faith as I for mine. And even though my name were appended to the declaration read to us by the gentleman from Mississippi, from the Pennsylvanian, I might still vote for such a man, if otherwise it lay in my way to do so.

I thank God and the honorable gentleman for that. I may think as I please on matters purely spiritual. But the gentleman proceeds

But there is another branch of this subject. It is a current belief that the Pope, the head of the Roman Church, who stands as the Vicar of God and is invested with His attributes of infallibility, is not only supreme in matters of faith but has also a temporal power that cannot only control governments, but, in fitting exigencies, may absolve his disciples from their allegiance. I am aware, sir, that this is disputed ground. But it is a well-attested historical fact, that often, in time past, the claim to secular power has been made; and I am yet to learn, that by the Pope, or any general council speaking with his acquiescence—the only authorized exponents of the true faith—that this claim has ever yet been disavowed. *It has not been done in England. . . .* I will say that, if it be true that the Pope is held to be supreme in secular, as in sacred affairs, that he can absolve men from their relations with others not of the true faith, it is not strange that men should hesitate in support of his followers. I would not vote for any man holding to that doctrine, and, I doubt not, other gentlemen here would concur with me in that feeling.

The charge then against the Roman Catholics of this country is, that their view of the supremacy of the Pope renders them unsafe citizens, because it renders them liable to be withdrawn from their allegiance to their own civil government by the decrees or ordinances of their spiritual superior. Of the cruelty of disturbing the public mind with such questions, and disfranchising well-disposed citizens, I shall not now speak. I shall leave to other times, and other persons, and in other places, too, the task of impeaching and of developing the motives upon which such discreditable and unrighteous pro-

ceedings rest. I shall leave to those who have
more bitterness of temper than I possess, to
show that, though newly revived, the charge is as
old as the hostility of Paganism to Christianity;
and that those who are vitiating public sentiment
in thus ministering to the appetite which they
have made morbid, have their prototype in the
malignants who would crucify the Saviour " lest
the Romans come and take our city from us," or
in the Titus Oats of later times, who disturbed
the public mind of England by discoveries of
plots that existed only in his infamous invention,
and who, by his perjuries, sent men to the scaffold whose innocence is now as generally admitted as is the corruption of the court in which
such fantastic tricks were played, and as the in-
famy of the wretch who could destroy the peace
of an excellent portion of the community, and
send to the scaffold and block men of immacu-
late purity, merely to give himself a temporary
notoriety, and a sort of political aggrandizement.
That branch of the discussion I turn from, with
loathing and disgust at the offensive details, and
with horror at its intimate association with the
men, the motives, and the means of modern
times. I leave such considerations to others,
and proceed to take notice of that part of the
subject which concerns the political relations of
American Catholics with the head of the Roman
Catholic Church—the character and fealty which
I, and all of the Catholic creed in this country,
owe to the Bishop of Rome.

The question raised by the gentleman from Massachusetts is one of political power, and that, I imagine, is the leading objection to Catholics and to Catholicity with gentlemen who venture on the dangerous movement of dragging religion into the political arena. Mr. Chairman, I deny that the Bishop of Rome has, or that he claims for himself, the right to interfere with the political relations of any other country than that of which he is himself the sovereign! I mean— and I have no desire to conceal any point—I mean that I deny to the Bishop of Rome the right resulting from his divine office, to interfere in the relations between subjects and their sovereigns, between citizens and their governments. And while I make this denial, I acknowledge all my obligations to the Church of which I am an humble member, and I recognize all the rights of the venerable head of that Church to the spiritual deference of its children; and I desire that no part of what I may say, or what I may concede, in my remarks, may be considered as yielding a single dogma of the Catholic Church, or manifesting, on my part, a desire to explain away, to suit the spirit of the times, or the prejudices of my hearers, any doctrine of the Catholic Church. I believe all that that Church believes and teaches as religious dogmas, but I am not bound by the imputations of its opponents. I am not bound by the assertions of those who would make political capital out of denunciations of her children, or misrepresentations of her creed. Nay, more, sir; and I ask the attention of gentlemen to my disavowal. I am not bound by any action which the Pope takes as a temporal sovereign, or which he performs as Bishop of Rome, or Pope, when he is only carrying out a contract with Kings and Emperors to secure to them the integrity of their possessions, and the perpetuity of their power.

As I cannot accept the honorable gentleman's discrimination between me, as a Catholic, and other members of the Church as Roman Catholics, I must regard myself as involved in the general censure, and feel that I stand charged, a national Representative, with holding opinions and owing fealty that may demand from me a sacrifice of patriotism to a higher obligation; pointed at, sir, as a man who, while he swears to maintain the Constitution of the country, and professes to make the fulfilment of his obligation to that country his paramount political duty, yet cherishes in his heart the principles of latent treason. I may be allowed, without the imputation of vanity, to make one more direct allusion to myself and my creed. And, sir, clearly and distinctly do I deny that the power of the Pope extends one grain beyond his spiritual relations with the members of his Church, or impinges, in the least degree, upon the political allegiance which any Roman Catholic of this country may owe to the Government and Constitution of the United States.

And, sir, that this disavowal of a divided

fealty may not be regarded as a mere generality, I give it explicitness by declaring that if, by any providence, the Bishop of Rome should become possessed of armies and a fleet, and, in a spirit of conquest, or any other spirit, should invade the territory of the United States, or assail the rights of our country, he would find no more earnest antagonists than the Roman Catholics. And for myself, if not here in this hall to vote supplies for a defending army, or if too old to take part in the active defense, I should, if alive, be at least in my chamber, or at the foot of the altar, imploring God for the safety of my country and the defeat of the invaders. (*Applause.*) /

THE CHAIRMAN (Mr. Orr) reminded the gentlemen that applause was not becoming in a deliberative body.

MR. CHANDLER. Or, if the spirit of conquest and cruelty should seize upon the wearer of the tiara, and he should seek to subjugate Italy by improper assumptions, and, by crime, provoke the arms of other nations against his own city, I could look on the chances of the defeat of his army as coolly and as complacently as on the misfortunes and punishment of any other ambitious monarch, and, safe in my love of right, and in the enjoyment of my religious creed, and the comforts of my home, I could say, " Let the Volscians plow Italy and harrow Rome."

Mr. Chairman, I do not wish to attract attention by declamation; I wish to state simply and distinctly, but very emphatically, what are the opinions of a Roman Catholic as to the influence of the dogma of Papal supremacy on political allegiance, and my own opinion I have given. But since some exception was made in my behalf, an exception which I cannot admit, though I thank the honorable gentleman for the courtesy with which it was expressed—and since it may be asserted that, as a Republican and layman, I could not be supposed to understand all the relations and influences of the dogma of the supremacy of the Pope, let me add, that what I assert as my belief of the entire political independence of every Roman Catholic out of the Papal States—political independence, I mean, of the Chief Magistrate of that State—is fully held and openly asserted and approved by every Catholic bishop and archbishop of the United States.

I have not time here to quote from the writings of all those who have published their opinions upon the subject, nor shall I have space to copy them in my published remarks, but I may say that such are the views which I have learned from them in conversation, and such is the view of the late Dr. England, a Roman Catholic Bishop of Charleston, a divine whose erudition and whose well-established fame gave cousequence to all he asserted, and whose zeal for the Church of which he was a distinguished prelate, and whose lofty position in the estimation of the Sovereign Pontiff rendered it unlikely that he would underrate the Papal power.

Extract from a letter of Bishop England to an Episcopal clergyman, Vol. II, pp. 250-51:

This charge which you make upon the Papists is exactly the same charge which the Jews were in the habit of making against the Apostles. From that day to the present we have met it as we meet it now. We have a kingdom, it is true, in which we pay no obedience to Cæsar; but our kingdom is not of this world—and whilst we render unto God the things that are God's, we render unto Cæsar the things that are Cæsar's. To the successors of the Apostles we render that obedience which is due to the authority left by Jesus Christ, who alone could bestow it. We do not give it to the President; we do not give it to the Governor; we do not give it to the Congress; we do not give it to the Legislature of the State—neither do you; nor do they claim it—nor would we give it, if they did, for the claim would be unfounded. We give to them everything which the Constitution requires; you give no more—you ought not to give more. Let the Pope and Cardinals, and all the powers of the Catholic world united, make the least encroachment on that Constitution, we will protect it with our lives. Summon a general council —let that council interfere in the mode of our electing but an assistant to a turnkey of a prison—we deny its right; we reject its usurpation. Let that council lay a tax of one cent only upon any of our churches; we will not pay it. Yet we are most *obedient Papists*— we believe the Pope is Christ's Vicar on earth, supreme visible head of the Church throughout the world, and lawful successor to St. Peter, Prince of the Apostles. We believe all this power is in Pope Leo XII, and we believe that a general council is infallible in doctrinal decisions. Yet we deny to Pope and council united any power to interfere with one tittle of our political rights, as firmly as we deny the power of interfering with one tittle of our spiritual rights to the President and Congress. We will obey each in its proper place, we will resist any encroachment by one upon the rights of the other. Will you permit Congress to do the duties of your convention? [2]

Here is another extract from the writings of the same Roman Catholic prelate:

Kings and Emperors of the Roman Catholic Church have frequently been at war with the Pope. Yet they did not cease to be members of the Church, and subject to his spiritual jurisdiction, although they resisted his warlike attacks. Any person in the least degree acquainted with the history of Europe, can easily refer to several instances. The distinction drawn by our Blessed Saviour, when he stood in the presence of Pilate, was the principle of those rulers. They were faithful to the head of the Church whose kingdom is not of this world but they repelled the attack of an enemy to their rights. You, sirs, acknowledge the authority of bishops. Suppose a bishop under whom you were placed, proceeded to take away your property; could you not defend your rights at law without infringing upon his spiritual authority? Are you reduced to the dilemma of being plundered or of denying an article of your religion? Can you not keep your property and deny the right of the bishop to take it away, and resist his aggression, at the same time that you are canonically obedient? Can you not be faithful to him as bishop, and to yourself as a man? Thus, suppose the Bishop of the Protestant Episcopal Church of Maryland claimed some right which he neither had by your Church law nor by the law of the State. You may, and ought to, resist the aggression. Yet you would not be unfaithful to him. Let the Pope be placed in the same predicament; I can be faithful to the Pope and to the government under which I live.

[2] Edit. 1849, J. Murphy & Co., Baltimore. — *Editor's note.*

I care not whether that government be administered by a Papist, by a Protestant, by a Jew, by a Mohammedan, or by a Pagan. It is, then, untrue to assert, as you have done, that a consistent Papist, and dutiful subject of a Protestant administration, must be incompatible.[3]

Dr. Kenrick, Archbishop of Baltimore, one of the most learned of the Roman Catholic Church, asserts, positively, that the temporal power of which we speak was never claimed by the Church, and he challenges the production of a single decree or definition in which this power was propounded as an article of faith. " Such," says the learned bishop, " does not exist." [4]

Dr. Troy, Archbishop of Dublin, in his Supplement to the Pastoral Instruction says: " The deposing power of Popes never was an article of faith, or a doctrine of the Catholic Church, nor was it ever proposed as such by any Council, or by any Popes themselves who exercised it." [5]

Archbishop Hughes, of New York, is equally explicit on this point. And I might fill volumes with citations to prove my position.

A Council of the Catholic Church in Baltimore has expressed the same idea in the most emphatic terms.

[3] Ibid, Vol. II, p. 231.—*Editor's note.*

[4] *The Primacy of the Apostolic See Vindicated*, by the Right Rev. Francis P. Kenrick, D.D., p. 333.—*Editor's note.*

[5] In foot-note at p. 333 of *The Primacy of the Apostolic See Vindicated.* Ed., 1838, Jas. Kay, Jr., & Bro., 122 Chestnut St., Philadelphia.—*Editor's note.*

Mr. Chairman, since I began to speak here, I have received a treatise, by Bishop Spalding, of Kentucky, on this very subject, sustaining my view. It is a timely and acceptable offering, by a lady in the gallery, to the spirit of truth, and her influence will assist to promote and reward attention throughout the House, as the woman's offering of ointment from the alabaster box was scattered over the head of the Author of truth, while its fragrance was diffused throughout the chamber in which the offering was made.

But I shall, of course, be asked, whence the boldness of the assertion against Catholics, and whence the readiness to believe the charges if they are altogether unfounded? Has not the Pope exercised the power of deposing monarchs, and thus of releasing subjects from their allegiance? Has not he interfered with the temporalities of a sovereign, and thus exercised a power sufficient to justify the apprehensions of the timid, and to give some appearance of probability to the assertions of the bold, reckless, and unprincipled party politician of the present and recent time?

Mr. Chairman, as a Christian man and an American legislator, I have nothing but truth to utter; and I scorn to utter less than the whole of the truth.

Undoubtedly the Pope has proceeded to dethrone kings, and thus to release subjects. History declares that more than one monarch has been made to descend from his throne by the edict of the Pope, and that the allegiance of his subjects has been transferred, by that edict, to a succeeding monarch, who, however he may have obtained his crown, might have been compelled to lay it down at the bidding of the same authority that deposed his predecessor.

If, then, the Pope has exercised such a right, may he not, should he ever have the power, renew that exercise?

That, I suppose, Mr. Chairman, depends entirely upon the foundation of the right, and the demand which may be made for its exercise.

The question which concerns us here, and which arises out of the charges made by the honorable gentleman from Massachusetts, is not whether the right has been claimed; but on what grounds this right was asserted. If it was a divine right—a right inherent in the *spiritual* office of the Bishop of Rome as the successor of St. Peter—then, sir, I confess it may never, it can never lapse; and its exercise may be renewed with the reception of additional power. But, sir, if it was a right conferred for special occasions, by those interested in its exercise, conferred by monarchs for their own safety, and approved by the people for their own benefit, who were ready, willing, and able to contribute means for giving its exhibition power, then it would, of course, cease with the change of circumstances in which it was conferred; and those who invested the Pope with the *right,* because they could assist him with *power,* and because general safety required the exercise of that power, retained in their own hands the right to withdraw or invalidate their former bestowal, and leave in the hands of the Roman Pontiff only his spiritual rights over kings or people, *dehors* the limits of his own temporal dominion.

To understand how the Pope ever possessed any power over emperors and kings, and by such power, influencing their subjects, we must enter more minutely into the circumstances of the far distant age in which it was conferred and exercised, than the time here allowed for a speech, or the space necessary for an essay, would justify. We must enter into the spirit of the Middle Ages, and see how naturally Christian monarchs (then all of one creed) formed combinations, and how much human rights and Christian principles owe to combinations; and jealousies which, while they distinguished, and really illustrated that period, would now be regarded, if they could exist, as the resort of men of bad principles, to perpetuate tyrannical power. But such was the state of the times, and such the unestablished condition of religion and civil government, that it became a matter of the deepest moment to Christian Princes, that the latter should combine to support the former. And in combining, the Christian (Catholic) Princes formed a league by which peace, order, and religion were, as far as possible, to be maintained among them by a reference to the influences which the Pope, as a spiritual sovereign, would naturally have to enforce temporal and temporary power with kings and people, and with kings through their people; and this influence was augmented by the submission on the part of individual sovereigns to the decrees of the Pope, founded on the power which the united sovereigns had conferred on the Pontiff, and founded on that alone.

Christianity, at that period, had not wrought out its work of social good; vice and disorder were rampant, and the passions of men seemed to be allowed indulgences little realized in these times. To secure something like order, religion, and catholicity, among the Christian nations, and to secure the ultimate social effects of the true principles of religion, the Christian princes conferred upon the Pope a power, which previously he had not attempted to exercise; never, indeed, claimed to possess. The spiritual power was always admitted as of divine right, the gift of God. The temporal power was conceded, was conferred, by the emperor and Christian princes, not to aggrandize the Bishop of Rome, but to enable him to decide betwixt them in their various disputes; and to keep alive the faith upon which the power of the princes evidently rested. No one then pretended that the right to depose a king was a divine right in the Pope. He claimed the power to cut off from the sacraments of the Church, all who did not conform to the rules of that Church, a right claimed and exercised by all churches, I suppose; as every

church surely must be a judge of the qualifica-
tions of its members, and must, so far as its influence extends, exercise the power to bind and
loose. That is a question purely theological, and
cannot be discussed here.

I certainly do no injustice to any one in saying
that such was the disorderly state of Europe,
that, if dependence had not been placed by sovereigns in the influence of the Pope's spiritual
power, no king could have maintained his possessions without an acknowledged physical su-
periority; and no people could have retained a
show of freedom, could have counted on life
itself, if the avarice and bloody cruelty of the
barons could have found any advantage or even
momentary gratification by sacrificing either.
And this was not all. It was admitted that
every crown should be held by the tenure of
Christianity in its wearer; and yet Paganism
and infidelity were continually grasping at the
sceptre.[6] Kingdoms were constantly changing.

[6] *The Foreign Quarterly,* for January, 1836, says:
" In the eleventh century the Papacy fought the battle
of freedom." [P. 221.—Ed.]

Ancellon, unfriendly to the Pope, says: " In the
Middle Ages, when there was no social order, it was
the influence and power of the Popes that, perhaps,
alone, saved Europe from the state of barbarism. . . .
It was their power that prevented and stayed the des-
potism of the emperors, that replaced the want of
equilibrium and diminished the inconveniences of the
feudal system." [Quoted in *Comparative View of the
Grounds of the Catholic and Protestant Churches.* By
the Rev. John Fletcher, D.D. Baltimore: Published

Monarchs were driven from their thrones by violence; and their successors rarely thought of any other object than the permanency of their own power. Meantime the Papacy was permanent; and, in proportion to the troubles, disorders, and disasters of the times, the Papacy acquired strength; strength in the constant appeals to its arbitration; strength in its unchangeable qualities, and strength, it will be admitted, by a reception and exercise of duties devolved upon it by those who saw in the Papal power the only means of saving Europe from chaos.

Having asserted that the political power of

by Fielding Lucas, Jr. J. Robinson, Printer. P. 157.—*Editor's note.*]

Southey says: "The Papacy . . . was morally and intellectually the conservative power of Christendom. Politically, too, it was the saving of Europe." [Ibidem, p. 157.—*Editor's note.*]

And a Protestant writer in the *American Encyclopedia,* in an article on Gregory VII, says: "The Papal power was for ages the great bulwark of order amid the turbulence of the semi-civilized people of Europe."

[This sentence is not found in the edition consulted by the present editor. But in *Chambers' Encyclopedia,* Vol. V, p. 412, ed. 1893, is the following, to the same purpose:

"By his firm and unbending efforts to suppress the un-Christian vices which deformed society and to restrain the tyranny which oppressed the subject as much as it enslaved the Church, he taught his age 'that there was a being on earth whose especial duty it was to defend the defenceless, to succour the succourless, to afford a refuge to the widow and orphan, and to be the guardian of the poor'."—*Editor's note.*]

25

the Popes, *dehors* their special and proper dominion, was conferred by the Christian princes,
and that it was exercised by the demands and
appeals of those who were interested in its object, viz. order, religion, and princely right, and
sometimes *popular* rights, I have only to say that
of course no Pope thus receiving and thus exercising his power could, with truth, assert a divine
right; or, asserting it, he could not hope to have
that right permanently admitted. It hence follows that such a right never was an article of
Roman Catholic faith.

It cannot be denied that the spiritual power
of the Pope, the admitted *jure divino,* was a
motive among others for conferring the political power, and, perhaps, also a motive for exercising that power; and the reverence in which
the character of the Pope was held by princes
and nobles, as well as the people, gave great consequence to the decisions of the Pontiff, right or
wrong, and insured prompt obedience, when
otherwise there might have been hesitancy and
even calcitration. No doubt, the temporal power
conferred by temporal consent and by a constitution, was mistaken for, and admitted by, certain weak persons at that time as the spiritual
power conferred by Christ, and sustained by the
Scriptures. But nowhere is the right to such a
power claimed, as of divine right, by the Catholic Church.

In the Catholic Church, as in all other
churches, there have been found a few individ-

uals of less discretion than zeal, who have, from a mistaken view of the Christian duties, thought it a merit on themselves to impute to religion a direct secular power which it never was intended by God, nor understood by good, prudent men, to exercise. We see it in the careless writings of certain Catholic scholars, as we find it in the preaching and discipline of many other denominations. But in the Catholic Church those individual opinions have been discountenanced by the bishops, and in other churches they have grown much out of practice; by all they are considered as rendering unto God the things which are Cæsar's. The assertion by individuals, or the practice by a few Popes, of any power, does not make that power right. That only is of faith which is so declared, and which is for all times and all circumstances.

The most distinguished instance of the exercise of the Papal power of deposing a monarch, is that by the Pope Gregory VII, who excommunicated and deposed the Emperor Henry IV. The peculiar character of these times I have already noticed. The peculiar character of Henry IV may be learned from history. He was corrupt, venal, turbulent, cruel, blasphemous, hypocritical. He had violated his coronation oath, and was engaged in enormities that drew, from every part of Germany and the north of Italy, appeals to the Pope for the exercise of those powers which the Pontiff held from the emperor; and when the Pope was exercising his admitted legal powers against the emperor, Henry called a council, and caused to be passed and promulgated a sentence of deposition against Gregory, the Pope. Of course, this drew from Rome a sentence of excommunication, and excommunication, unless removed within a year, was to assist in working out *depositions*. The Princes of Germany, even, assembled to elect a successor to Henry; but the excommunicated emperor, in full acknowledgment of the power of the Pope, hastened to Italy, made submission, saved himself from dethronement, returned to his German home, fourfold more a child of the devil than he had been, was deposed, and died a miserable outcast. Though those events took place at a time and under circumstances when little regard was paid to the niceties of temporal distinctions, yet the Pope (Gregory) did not claim that his action in deposing the emperor was by divine right, because he knew, and all knew that, by a law of the empire, Henry had forfeited the imperial throne, and that the Pope was as much authorized to depose him for violating a law of the empire as he was to excommunicate him for open violation of the commands of God and the Church.

In a letter [7] from Gregory VII to the German Lords, he, the Pope, expressly declares that he did not pretend to ground himself merely on the

[7] Paul Bernried, *De Rebus gestis Gregorii VII*, Cap. lxxvii, apud Gosselin, *Power of Pope in the Middle Ages.—Editor's note.*

divine power of binding and loosing, but on the laws of men—that is, the constitution or laws of the empire, as well as the laws of God; and, according to the last-named code, as well as the requirement of the former, Henry deserved, not only to be excommunicated, but also to be deposed of his imperial dignity.

The most distinguished writer [8] of the time of Gregory VII, Peter Damien, shows that Gregory did not depend alone upon his spiritual power, but acted upon the authority of the constitution of the empire. If Gregory had claimed, and others had admitted a divine right *alone* to depose an emperor, his apologist would scarcely, at such a time, have presented the smaller right of human authority.

The following, from a work on the temporal power of the Pope, by Mr. Gosselin, [9] is directly to the point, and will illustrate this part of my remarks:

From these observations it follows, in fact, first, that Gregory VII, the first that ever pronounced a sentence of deposition against a sovereign, did not pretend to ground his proceeding solely on the divine right, but on laws both human and divine. Secondly, that in the opinion of Gregory VII, and of his suc-

[8] Probably Peter Damien, a friend and contemporary of Gregory VII. Works found in Migue's *Patr. Lat.,* Vols. CXLIV and CXLV. See Gosselin, Vol. II, p. 191.—*Editor's note.*

[9] *The Power of Pope in the Middle Ages,* M. Gosselin, Vol. II, p. 292. English translation by Matthew Kelly, London, 1853, C. Dolman.—*Editor's note.*

cessors, as well as of all their contemporaries, the deposition of an excommunicated Prince was not a necessary consequence of excommunication, and did not follow from the divine power of binding and loosing alone, but from a special provision of a human law, and principally from the laws of the Empire, which declared deposed of his throne any Prince remaining obstinately under excommunication during a whole year.

These important facts once proved, there is no difficulty in understanding how the Popes could naturally cite, in support of their sentences of excommunication and deposition against Princes, the divine power of binding and loosing, though not considering it as the sole title of that deposing power which they claimed. It is, in fact, evident that, at a time when constitutional law attached the penalty of deposition to excommunication or heresy, the Pope's sentence against such excommunicated or heretical Prince was grounded both on the divine right and on human law. It was founded on the divine right, not merely in so far as it declared the Prince heretical or excommunicated, but still more, in so far as it enlightened the conscience of his subjects on the extent and limits of the obligation arising from the oath of allegiance which they had taken to him. It was founded on human law also, in so far as it declared the Prince deprived of his rights, in punishment of his remaining obstinately in heresy or excommunication. It is obvious, also, why the Pope's sentence mentioned only the divine power of binding and loosing, for it was on that divine power that the sentence was really grounded, considered in its principal, direct, and immediate object; for the deposition was effected by excommunication— its natural result, according to the constitutional law then in force.

While I have asserted, and, with the little time

allowed me, referred you to the authorities upon which my assertions rest, that the Popes of the Middle Ages did not declare that their interference with the temporal powers of kings and emperors was authorized by their spiritual commissions, as Bishops of Rome; and that their antagonistic and summary proceedings toward offending sovereigns, with regard to the temporal powers of the latter were authorized by a constitution formed by these sovereigns or their predecessors, I do not pretend to assert that the power was always rightly used. I do not deny ambitious or vengeful motives to the Popes. Nothing in my creed or theirs presents such a conclusion, and nothing in their conduct renders such a conclusion unreasonable. I only say that the spiritual power *here* is not in question, and there, and at that time the power to depose—power humanly conferred—was never called in question by the deposed monarchs. They admitted the constitutional right and power, though they may have called in question the justice of the act. With the justice of the proceeding I have nothing to do here, though I may be allowed to say that, however the Pope may have transgressed the rules of justice as between him and the deposed monarch, it is probable that, as between the monarch and the people, there was little occasion to suppose that any injustice had been done to the prince, or much likelihood of hearing complaints from the latter. The Pope has struggled sometimes with sovereigns, but never with the sovereignty. He has exercised a power voluntarily placed in his hands by kings, and invoked by the people; and he has dethroned the monarch, but not anathametized the subject. The Popes, in the fulfilment of what the consent of kings and the confidence of the people have made a duty, have released subjects from the oath of allegiance to the sovereign, but never have they released the sovereign from his coronation oath to respect, guard, and rightly govern the people.

Because I have neither time nor space for such an inquiry, I do not pursue the subject in detail. I have taken the strongest case of the exercise of the power of deposing monarchs— which is now called the power of releasing subjects—and I have shown that the Pope did not rely upon the general spiritual power as head of the Christian Church for authority to depose the emperor, but that he rested on, and was sustained by, the constitution which authorized the election of an emperor, and made orthodoxy one condition of holding the crown. And it would have been equally easy, generally less difficult, to have shown that every instance of such exercise of power by the Pope was authorized by the admitted constitution or acknowledged compact, provided that the offenses of the Prince had brought him within the operation of the laws, which all admitted to exist, and for the execution of which all turned to the Pope.

Now, as this kind of secular power had its

origin in the consent of the sovereigns, at a particular time, and long after the Apostolic age, it follows that not only could it not have carried with it the *jure divino*, which belongs to the spiritual power of the Bishop of Rome, but that the proof of the existence of the real spiritual power would have been weakened by attempts to prove the right of deposing to be divine. At that time, then—at a time when men were most willing to yield assent to such species of usurpation, as released kings from a bad emperor, and relieved subjects from bad kings—at that time the divine right was not claimed, and the whole power of deposing rested upon the consent, not merely of the kings, but of the deposed princes themselves.

But it is charged that Roman Catholics even now admit the right of the Pope to interfere between subjects and their allegiance, and between citizens and their duties to the Republic, in some other form, since the power to depose kings is no longer possible. I deny it; I have denied it for myself plainly, clearly, specifically. But, in this House, it is said that, though I may be excepted from the general censure of harboring the seeds and means of treason to this Government in my breast, and warming them into germination by devotion, yet others are liable to the charge, and especially the Church, the Roman Catholic Church itself.

But the Roman Catholic Church is represented by her bishops, and therefore I turn to the statements of those having the means of knowing,

33

and the right to make known the doctrines of that Church and ask the attention of the Committee to the following remarks of the Right Rev. Dr. England:

God never gave to St. Peter any temporal power, any authority to depose kings, any authority to interfere with political concerns. And rights which his successors might claim for any of those purposes must be derived from some other source. A Roman Catholic has no further connexion with the Pope than that he succeeds St. Peter. Peter had none of these rights—as a Roman Catholic, I know nothing of them in the Pope. He is equally a Pope, with or without them.[10]

In the early part of my remarks, I took occasion to say what would be my course, if, by any remarkable (but really impossible) concurrence of circumstances, the army and navy of the Pope should invade the country. Hear now how the Bishop of Charleston sustains my declaration:

The American Constitution leaves its citizens in perfect freedom to have whom they please to regulate their spiritual concerns. But if the Pope were to declare war against America, and any Roman Catholic, under the pretext of spiritual obedience, was to refuse to oppose this temporal aggressor, he would deserve to be punished for his refusal, because he owes to this country to maintain its rights; and spiritual power does not, and cannot, destroy the claim which the government has upon him. Suppose a clergyman of England were convicted of some crime—for instance Dr. Dodd—and he was ordered for execution; must the

[10] Vol. III, p. 176. Edition of Arthur Clark, Cleveland, Ohio, 1908.—*Editor's note.*

law be inoperative because the criminal is a clergyman? Think you that no one could be found in a Roman Catholic country to sentence, or to execute a sentence, upon a clergyman who was a criminal? All history testifies to the contrary. So too does all history show that upon the same principle, Catholic kings and princes, and peers, and people, have disobeyed improper mandates of the See of Rome, and have levied and carried on war against Popes, and still continued members of the Church.[11]

Mr. Chairman, I have thus shown that the Church, in the Middle Ages, did not claim for the Popes the authority to exercise temporal power over other sovereigns, by divine right, even when the exercise of that authority seemed to be so great a blessing to the people that it would scarcely seem wonderful if the people should have hailed it as of divine origin. And I have shown that the best writers of the Catholic Church, of later days, and of the present century, have, in like manner, denied, that it was part of a Catholic's belief that the Pope possesses any power to depose kings, or release subjects, or to violate faith with those who are or are not of the Catholic Church. I now offer other proof that the Church sets up no claim to such power. And, before I do it, I may be permitted to say that, in the pursuit of information with regard to the Catholic Church, it has been my chance to converse with every rank and degree of her hierarchy—Pope, Cardinal, Nuncio, Archbishop, Bishop, and Priest, and I never

[11] Ibid.—*Editor's note.*

35

heard one of them claim any such power, and never heard one of them speak upon the subject who did not disavow any belief of its existence.

The vexed question of governing Ireland, and of granting to the people of that kingdom a part of the rights enjoyed by the subjects of Great Britain, has often lead the British Parliament to inquire into the charges made against the Roman Catholics, with reference to the asserted right of the Roman Pontiff to interfere with the internal affairs of other Governments.

Three propositions were prepared and sent to the faculties of the principal Catholic Universities in France and Spain; those of the University of Paris, of Douay, of Louvain, of Acala, of Salamanca, and of Valladolid. I give the propositions and abstracts of the several answers.

Extracts from the declarations and testimonies of six of the principal Universities of Europe on the three following propositions, submitted to them at the request of Mr. Pitt, by the Catholics of London, in 1789:

THE PROPOSITIONS.[12]

1. Has the Pope, or Cardinals, or any body of men, or any individual of the Church of Rome, any civil authority, power, jurisdiction, or preëminence whatsoever, within the realm of England?

2. Can the Pope, or Cardinals, or any body of men,

---

[12] *An Historical Review of the State of Ireland*, by Francis Plowden; Philadelphia, 1806; Vol. IV, Appendix, p. 27; also Butler's *English Catholics.—Editor's note.*

or any individual of the Church of Rome, absolve or dispense with his Majesty's subjects from their oath of allegiance, upon any pretext whatsoever?

3. Is there any principle in the tenets of the Catholic faith by which Catholics are justified in not keeping faith with heretics, or other persons differing from them in religious opinions, in any transaction, either of a public or a private nature?

These propositions, honorable gentlemen will perceive, are skilfully drawn, and cover the whole ground of dispute; and the answer of every University addressed, is spread at large before the world. Solemn deliberation was had upon the propositions, from so respectable a source as Mr. Pitt, and all concur in declaring that no man nor any body of men, of the Church of Rome, however assembled, has power to interfere with the affairs of other kingdoms. I give the answers.

After an introduction, according to the usual forms, the sacred faculty of Divinity of Paris, answers *the first query* by declaring:

Neither the Pope, nor the Cardinals, nor any body of men, nor any other person of the Church of Rome, hath *any* civil authority, civil power, civil jurisdiction, or civil preëminence whatsoever in any kingdom; and, consequently, none in the kingdom of England, by reason or virtue of any authority, power, jurisdiction, or preëminence by divine institution inherent in, or granted, or by an other means belonging to the Pope or the Church of Rome. This doctrine the sacred faculty of divinity of Paris has always held, and upon every occasion maintained, and upon every occasion has rigidly proscribed the contrary doctrines from her schools.

adversaries in imputing this tenet to them, etc., etc., etc.

Given at Paris, in the general assembly of the Sorbonne, held on Thursday, the eleventh day before the kalends of March, 1789.

Signed in due form.

UNIVERSITY OF DOUAY, 5 JANUARY, 1789.

At a meeting of the faculty of Divinity of the University of Douay, etc., etc., etc.

To the first and second queries the sacred faculty answers: that no power, whatsoever, in civil or temporal concerns, was given by the Almighty, either to the Pope, the Cardinals, or the Church herself, and, consequently, that kings and sovereigns are not, in temporal concerns, subject, by the ordination of God, to any ecclesiastical power whatsoever; neither can their subjects, by any authority granted, to the Pope or the Church, from above, be freed from their obedience or absolved from their oath of allegiance.

This is the doctrine which the Doctors and Professors of Divinity hold and teach in our schools, and

38

this all the candidates for degrees in Divinity maintain in their public theses, etc., etc.

To the third question, the sacred faculty answers: that there is no principle of the Catholic faith, by which Catholics are justified in not keeping faith with heretics who differ from them in religious opinions. On the contrary, it is the *unanimous doctrine* of Catholics that the respect due to the name of God, so called to witness, requires that the oath be inviolably kept, to whomsoever it is pledged, whether Catholic, heretic, or infidel, etc., etc.

Signed and sealed in due form.

UNIVERSITY OF LOUVAIN.

The faculty of Divinity at Louvain, having been requested to give her opinion upon the questions above stated, does it with readiness—but struck with astonishment that such questions should, at the end of this, the eighteenth century, be proposed to any learned body, by inhabitants of a kingdom that glories in the talents and discernment of its natives. The faculty being assembled for the above purpose, it is agreed, with the unanimous assent of all voices to answer the first and second queries absolutely in the negative.

The faculty does not think it incumbent upon her in this place to enter upon the proofs of her opinion, or to show how it is supported by passages in the Holy Scriptures, or the writings of antiquity. That has already been done by Bossuet, De Marca, the two Barclays, Goldastus, the Pitæacuses, Argentre Widrington, and his Majesty King James I, in his dissertation against Bellarmine, and Du Perron, and many others, etc.

The faculty then proceeds to declare that the sovereign power of the State is in no wise (not even indirectly, as it is termed) subject to or dependent upon, any other power, though it be a spiritual power, or even though it be instituted for eternal salvation, etc.

That no man, nor any assembly of men, however eminent in dignity and power, not even the whole body of the Catholic Church, though assembled in general Council, can, upon any ground, or pretense whatsoever, weaken the bond of union between the sovereign and the people; still less can they absolve or free the subjects from their oath of allegiance.

Proceeding to the third question, the said faculty of Divinity (in perfect wonder that such a question should be proposed to her) most positively and unequivocally answers:

That there is not, and there never has been, among the Catholics, or in the doctrines of the Church of Rome, any law or principle which makes it lawful for Catholics to break their faith with heretics, or others of a different persuasion from themselves, in matters of religion, either in public or private concerns.

The faculty declares the doctrines of the Catholics to be, that the divine and natural law, which makes it a duty to keep faith and promises, is the same, and is neither shaken nor diminished, if those with whom the engagement is made, hold erroneous opinions in matters of religion, etc., etc.

Signed in due form, on the 18th of November, 1788.

UNIVERSITY OF ALCALA.

To the first question, it is answered: that none of the persons mentioned in the proposed question, either individually or collectively, in council assembled, have any right in civil matters; but that all civil power, jurisdiction, and preëminence, are derived from Inheritance, election, the consent of the people, and other such titles of that nature.

To the second, it is answered in like manner: that

none of the persons above mentioned have a power to absolve the subjects of his Britannic Majesty from their oaths of allegiance.

To the third question, it is answered: that the doctrine which would exempt Catholics from the obligation of keeping faith with heretics, or with any other persons who dissent from them in matters of religion, instead of being an article of Catholic faith, is entirely repugnant to its tenets.

Signed in the usual form, 17 March, 1789.

UNIVERSITY OF SALAMANCA.

To the first question, it is answered: that neither Pope nor Cardinals, nor any assembly or individual of the Catholic Church, have as such, any civil authority, power, jurisdiction, or preëminence in the kingdom of England.

To the second, it is answered: that neither Pope nor Cardinals, nor any assembly or individual of the Catholic Church, can, as such, absolve the subjects of Great Britain from their oaths of allegiance, or dispense with its obligations.

To the third, it is answered: that it is no article of Catholic faith, not to keep faith with heretics, or with persons of any other description, who dissent from them in matters of religion.

Signed in the usual form, 7 March, 1789.

UNIVERSITY OF VALLADOLID.

To the first question, it is answered: that neither Pope, cardinals, or even a general council, have any civil authority, power, jurisdiction, or preëminence, directly or indirectly, in the kingdom of Great Britain, or over any other kingdom or province in which they possess no temporal dominion.

To the second, it is answered: that neither pope nor cardinals, nor even a general council can absolve the subjects of Great Britain from their oaths of allegiance or dispense with their obligation.

41

To the third, it is answered: that the obligation of keeping faith is grounded on the law of nature, which binds all men equally, without respect to their religious opinions; and with regard to Catholics, it is still more cogent, as it is confirmed by the principles of their religion.

Signed in the usual form, 17 February, 1789.

Can anything be more explicit than the responses of these Universities? Ought they not to be satisfactory? I, perhaps, ought to rest here. Layman, Priest, Bishop, Cardinal, and faculty of Divinity sustain my assertion, give a negative response to every query that involved an implication upon the patriotism of Catholics, or an inadmissible claim to intervention in national policy by the Catholic Church.

So entirely satisfied was the British Parliament with these and similar responses, that the different concessions made to Roman Catholics by that body was mainly due to such testimony.

And, let it be remembered, that this was in Great Britain, in a British Parliament, where the members were of the Established Church, and also that, without special permission, no man in that empire had a right to worship God according to the dictates of his own conscience, and none, not acknowledging in the monarch of England (man or woman, king or queen) both temporal and spiritual sovereignty, could hold an office under Government, or sit in the Parliament of the nation.

We, Mr. Chairman, are legislating for a country where even toleration may be deemed intolerant, where perfect equality of rights is the theory of the Government, and where, until now, no one has ventured to manifest a hostility to another's creed, by denying to him the right of national office, and of enjoying all the rights which full and perfect citizenship confers.

But the honorable gentleman from Massachusetts seems to have provided himself against such proof as I have adduced. He admits my fealty to the country, but denies my adherence to the Roman Catholic Church. He admits that France and Spain have disclaimed the doctrine against which he speaks, and which he imputes to the Roman Catholic Church. France and Spain, the titles of whose monarchs are most Christian and most Catholic! The honorable gentleman surely cannot be ignorant that such Universities—great theological colleges as those, are repositories of records of faith, and of the arguments and decisions concerning them. But let us hear the honorable gentleman:

MR. BANKS.—I plant myself upon the ground that the Pontiff of Rome has never, in any authoritative form, so disavowed the right to control the members of the Roman Catholic Church in secular matters. I know the universities of France and Spain have disclaimed that power. The gentleman says that his Catholic friends have disclaimed it to him. So my Catholic friends have disclaimed it to me. But they have not the right to private opinion, much less the right to determine the faith of their Church. That is the right of Protestants. The Roman Church has *never* disclaimed it.

43

I pass over the slur about private judgment; it is undeserved and might be retaliated. The honorable gentleman then suspecting that Laymen, Priests, and Bishops, would declare that the Church had no such articles of faith as he imputes, and being informed of the existence of those responses of the French and Spanish Universities, throws himself upon the Pope. " I plant myself," says he, " on the ground that the Pontiff of Rome has never, in any authoritative form, so disavowed the right to control the members of the Roman Catholic Church in secular affairs." Very well. He plants himself on what he calls a fact. Let us see how he is sustained. Let us proceed up from Layman to Priest, from Priest to Bishop, from Bishop to Archbishop, from Archbishop to Universities. These are all against the honorable gentleman, and, accepting the invitation or challenge of the gentleman from Massachusetts, let us plant ourselves upon the Pope himself, the Pope and his conclave of Cardinals.

Mr. Chairman, the same circumstance which induced that great statesman, Mr. Pitt, to address the six Catholic Universities, led the Roman Catholic Archbishops of Ireland to address the Pope himself on the subject, and the answer was as clear and explicit as those of the Universities. Solemn deliberation was given in the congregation of Cardinals, and the response was made in the most formal manner, as declaring the doctrine of the Catholic Church on the subject involved in the questions. I copy from an authentic report:

The Roman Catholic Archbishops of Ireland, at their meeting in Dublin, in 1791, addressed a letter to the Pope, wherein they described the misrepresentations that had been recently published of their consecration oath, and the great injury to the Catholic body arising from them. . . .

After due deliberation at Rome, the congregation of Cardinals appointed to superintend the ecclesiastical affairs of these kingdoms, returned an answer (of which the following is an extract) by the authority and command of His Holiness:

MOST ILLUSTRIOUS AND MOST REVEREND LORDS AND BROTHERS:

We perceive from your late letter, the great uneasiness you labor under since the publication of a pamphlet entitled *The Present State of the Church of Ireland,* from which our detractors have taken occasion to renew the old calumny against the Catholic religion with increased acrimony; namely: *that this religion is, by no means, compatible with the safety of Kings and Republics; because, as they say, the Roman Pontiff, being the father and master of all Catholics, and invested with such great authority, that he can free the subjects of other kingdoms from their fidelity and oaths of allegiance to Kings and Princes;* he has it in his power, they contend, to cause disturbances and injure the public tranquility of kingdoms with ease. We wonder that you could be uneasy at these complaints, especially after your most excellent brother and apostolic fellow-laborer, the Archbishop of Cashel, and other strenuous defenders of the rights of the Holy See, had evidently refuted and explained away these slanderous reproaches in their celebrated writings. In this controversy a most accurate discrimination should be made between the genuine rights of the Apostolic

See, and those that are imputed to it by innovators of this age for the purpose of calumniating. *The See of Rome never taught that faith is not to be kept with the heterodox: that an oath to Kings separated from the Catholic Communion, can be violated: that it is lawful for the Bishop of Rome to invade their temporal rights and dominions. We, too, consider an attempt or design against the life of Kings and Princes, even under the pretext of religion, as a horrid and detestable crime. . .*

At the very commencement of the yet infant Church, blessed Peter, Prince of the Apostles, instructing the faithful, exhorted them in these words: *Be ye subject to every human creature for God's sake, whether it be to the King as excelling, or to governors as sent by him for the punishment of evil-doers, and for the praise of the good: for so is the will of God, that by doing well you may silence the ignorance of foolish men.* The Catholic Church being directed by these precepts, the most renowned champions of the Christian name replied to the Gentiles, when raging against them, as enemies of the Empire, with furious hatred: *we are constantly praying* (Tertullian in Apologet., chap. xxx) *that all the Emperors may enjoy long life, quiet government, a loyal household, a brave army, a faithful Senate, an honest people, and general tranquility.* The Bishops of Rome, successors of Peter, have not ceased to inculcate this doctrine, especially to missionaries, lest any ill will should be excited against the professors of the Catholic faith in the minds of those who are enemies of the Christian name. We pass over the illustrious proofs of this fact, preserved in the records of ancient Roman Pontiffs, of which yourselves are not ignorant. We think proper, notwithstanding, to remind you of a late admonition of the most wise Pope Benedict XIV, who, in his regulations for the English missions, which are likewise applicable to you, speaks thus: *The Vicars Apostolic are to take diligent care that the missionaries behave on all occasions with integrity and decorum, and thus become good models to*

46

*others; and particularly that they be always ready to
celebrate the sacred offices, to communicate proper in-
structions to the people, and to comfort the sick with
their assistance; that they, by all means, avoid public
assemblies of idle men and taverns. . . The Vicars
themselves are particularly charged to punish in such
manner as they can, but severely, all those who do not
speak of the public government with respect.*

England herself can witness the deep-rooted impres-
sions such admonitions have made on the minds of
Catholics. It is well known that, in the late war, which
had extended to the greater part of America, when
most flourishing provinces, inhabited almost by persons
separated from the Catholic Church, had renounced the
Government of the King of Great Britain, the Province
of Canada alone, filled, as it is, almost with innumer-
able Catholics, although artfully tempted, and not yet
forgetful of the French Government, remained most
faithful in its allegiance to England. Do you, most
excellent prelates, converse frequently on these principles; often remind your suffragant prelates of them;
when preaching to your people, exhort them, again and
again, *to honor all men, to love the brotherhood, to
fear God, to honor the King.*

Those duties of a Christian are to be cherished in
every Kingdom and State, but particularly in your own,
of Great Britain and Ireland, where, from the benevo-
lence of a most wise King, and other most excellent
rulers of those Kingdoms, towards Catholics, no cruel
and grievous burden is imposed, and Catholics themselves experience a mild and gentle Government. If
you pursue this line of conduct unanimously; if you
act in the spirit of charity; if, while you direct the
people of the Lord, you have nothing in view but the
salvation of souls, adversaries will be ashamed (we
repeat it) to calumniate, and will freely acknowledge
that the Catholic faith is of heavenly descent, and cal-
culated not only to procure a blessed life, but likewise,
as St. Augustine observes, in his one hundredth and

thirty-eighth letter, addressed to Marcellinus, to promote the most lasting peace of this earthly city, inas-
much as it is the safest prop and shield of Kingdom.
Let those who say (the words are those of the holy
doctor) *that the doctrine of Christ is hostile to the Re-*
public, produce an army of such soldiers as the doctrine
of Christ has required; let them furnish such inhabi-
tants of provinces, such husbands, such wives, such
parents, such children, such masters, such servants,
such Kings, such judges, finally, such payers of debts
and collectors of the revenue, as the doctrine of Christ
enjoins, and then they may dare to assert that it is
inimical to the Republic—rather let them not hesitate
to acknowledge that it is, when practised, of great ad-
vantage to the Republic. The same holy doctor and
all the other fathers of the Church, with one voice,
most clearly demonstrate, by invincible arguments, that
the whole of this salutary doctrine cannot exist with
permanent consistency and stability, or flourish except in the Catholic society, which is spread and preserved all over the world, by communion with the See
of Rome, as a sacred bond of union, divinely connect-
ing both. From our very high esteem and affection for
you, we earnestly wish that the great God may very
long preserve you safe. Farewell.

As your lordship's most affectionate brother,

L. *Cardinal* ANTONELLI, *Prefect.*

A. ARCHBISHOP OF ADEN, *Secretary.*

Rome, 23 June, 1791.[13]

While on the disavowal of the Pope, I may
as well make an addition to assist in the testimony. The following document was drawn up

---

[13] Cf. Hergenröther, *Catholic Church and Christian*
State, London, 1876; reference to Vol. 18 of *Ami de la*
Religion, p. 198; also Affré, *Essai sur la Suprématie*
temporelle du Pape, p. 508; Paris, 1829.—*Editor's note.*

by the Roman Catholic Committee in Dublin, and published by them on the 17th of March, 1792, after it had been submitted to the Archbishops and Bishops of Ireland, and received their entire sanction. To give it greater weight, the same instrument was put into the form of an oath, retaining, as far as possible, the very words. It was then submitted to the Pope and Cardinals, who solemnly declared that it was consonant to, and expressive of, the Roman Catholic doctrine; and then it was taken by the Catholic archbishops, bishops, priests, and laity of Ireland.

We, the Catholics of Ireland . . . in deference to the opinion of many respectable bodies and individuals among our Protestant brethren, do hereby, in the face of our country, of all Europe, and before God, make this, our deliberate and solemn declaration.

1. We abjure, disavow, and condemn the opinion, that Princes excommunicated by the Pope and council, or *by any ecclesiastical authority whatsoever,* may, therefore, be deposed or murdered by their subjects, or by any other persons. We hold such doctrine in detestation, as wicked and impious, and we declare that we do not believe that either the Pope, with or without the general council, or *any prelate or priest, or any ecclesiastical power whatsoever,* can absolve the subjects of this kingdom, or any of them, from their allegiance to his Majesty King George III, who is, by authority of Parliament, the lawful King of this realm.

2. We abjure, condemn, and detest as unchristian and impious, the principle that it is lawful to murder, or destroy, or anywise injure any person whatsoever, for or under the pretense of being heretics; and we declare solemnly before God, that we believe *no act in itself unjust, immoral, or wicked, can ever be justified*

49

or excused by or under the pretense or color that it was done either for the good of the Church, or in obedience to any ecclesiastical power whatsoever.

3. We further declare, that we hold it an unchristian and impious principle, that " no faith is to be kept with heretics." This doctrine we detest and reprobate, not only as *contrary* to our religion, but as destructive of morality, of society, and even of common honesty; and it is our firm belief, that an *oath* made to any person not of the Catholic religion, is equally binding as if it were made to any Catholic whatsoever.

4. We have been charged with holding, as an article of our belief, that the Pope, with or without a general council, or that certain ecclesiastical powers, can acquit or absolve us before God from our oaths of allegiance, or even from the just oaths or contracts entered into between man and man.

Now we do utterly renounce, abjure, and deny that we hold or maintain any such belief, as being contrary to the peace and happiness of society, inconsistent with morality, and above all, *repugnant to the true spirit of the Catholic religion.* [14]

Here, then, is another clear, explicit disavowal on the part of the Pope and his Cardinals of the doctrine imputed to the Church, and another full and complete response to the challenge of the gentleman from Massachusetts.

Mr. Chairman, the Roman Catholic Church neither holds nor inculcates a doctrine of power in its head to interfere in the affairs of temporal Governments, to disturb the monarch, or release the subject. It never has held any such

[14] Plowden, op. cit., Vol. IV, Appendix, p. 8; also England, op. cit., Vol. III, p. 418; ed. 1908.—*Editor's note.*

doctrine. It never has taught that its professors were to be influenced by its doctrines to combine against the Government, and Catholic citizens have been as faithful to the Government under which they lived as those of any other denomination of Christians. In this country, Mr. Chairman, where, by the nature of our institutions, no creed is allowed to be molested, and where, by constitutional provision, no advantage can be allowed the professors of a creed on account of that profession, how unjust is it to the public, how cruel to the confessors of a creed, to create and keep alive an excitement which involves in obloquy a large class of citizens invested with every right that any American citizen can claim, who are able, by their talents, character, attainments, and patriotism, to do honor to the citizenship which they are not allowed to enjoy. I must not be told that " all the rights of citizenship are open to Catholics," when office is denied. The man who asserts that, is ignorant of the first impulse of republicanism—ignorant, I venture to say, of the strongest motives of his own action.

The right of suffrage is connected with the right of office, and the freeman's privilege of voting for the man whom he would elect, would be not worth the exercise, if it did not include the right of presenting himself for votes for any office whose functions are not beyond his faculties.

Form a class of citizens, sir, in this country,

with any disability not imposed upon others, and you create a dangerous party in the Commonwealth. Inequality of political conditions can only be maintained where there is inequality of mind, talents, and attainments. Allow to any class in this country the rights of education, the attainment of wealth, the right of social equality, of suffrage, and it will not be long before that class will demand the boon that freeman seek, and denial will be unsafe.

It is mean, it is cowardly, as well as false, for any man, or set of men, to assert that, in combining to exclude all Catholics from office, they do no more than exercise the right not to vote for individuals, which is as clear as the right to vote for them.

Sir, if the opposition seen and felt abroad, and heard here, in this Hall, means anything more than a miserable, beggarly appeal to low prejudices, with a view of holding office, it means that Catholics ought to be excluded from all office; and if they are, because they are Catholics, ineligible to place, then, those who assert it are bound to change the Constitution, or openly violate its provisions. Will that be done? Will they have courage to do it? They must do it to be consistent. They must forbear to be honest—a much more difficult effort.

Will that be done, and the question of the constitutional rights settled? or shall the Catholic Christian hear himself insulted, as he has been more than once here, with the offensive imputation which I have endeavored to refute? Shall the heart of the American Catholics be wounded with stale rumors—rumors revived for party action—uncredited tales to their dishonor, or hypothetical charges of concealed treason, which, while it ventures upon no specification, disturbs the public mind, awakens slumbering prejudices, sharpens religious animosities, and gives occasion for the mean, the ignorant, and the vulgar ambitious to rise into power, by the combination of their own class with those who, failing in other combinations, hide their disgrace, and avenge their former defeat by such associations as make minorities contemptible in themselves, and render majorities dangerous to the Republic.

Mr. Chairman, one word more and I will close. I have fairly and fully met the accusations made by the honorable gentleman from Massachusetts, against the Church of which I am a member. Step after step he retreated, until he had planted himself on the Bishop of Rome; and there he challenged the citation of a single disavowal on the part of the Pontiff, that he claimed temporal power over the subjects of other Governments. Step by step I have followed him, and concluded the array of disavowals by a presentation to this committee of an explicit denial on the part of the Pope that any such authority or right was claimed by the Church or by him.

Mr. Chairman, to the warnings expressed here, and the nervous apprehensions expressed abroad, that the prevalence of the Catholic religion will be dangerous to the country, I have only to say, that we of this country are in no danger from Catholicity, Episcopacy, Calvinism, Lutheranism, or other forms of Christianity. Sir, Christianity in any form is better than Infidelity and Atheism. And Atheism is now at work, as it ever has been busy, against the Christian faith and Christian prohibitions. It assails the Roman Catholic first, because that creed is more extensive; and without considering the evil which each is doing to religion, Christian men are yielding themselves, unconsciously, co-workers with infidelity by their active hostility to each other.

Mr. Chairman, if this country is to fall by any other means than ordinary decay or local convulsions, it is not Christianity, not the Christianity of Geneva, Rome, Scotland, or England, that will produce the ruin. The mischief will be wrought by infidelity. Sapping first the confidence of the people in each other, undermining the foundations of Christian charity, breaking the bonds of social life, relaxing the ties of moral obligations, setting creeds in hostile attitudes, till there is nothing left for hostility, and bringing down the whole scheme of domestic, social, and political life to the plans and ends of Socialists and Atheists, who laugh at the existence of a God, and seek their triumphs in the obliteration of the doctrines and teachings of Christ.

Mr. Chairman, I have forborne to-day all retaliatory imputations, all irritating comparisons,
and confided myself to a refutation of a charge
made against men of the Roman Catholic creed.
I have not sought this contest, but, for the sake
of honor, of truth, of myself and my co-religionists, for the sake of the institutions and the Constitution of my country, I could not decline it.
I have evaded no point, nor attempted to darken
counsel. I have met the charge fairly, candidly,
and truthfully. I have dealt in no street rumors.
I have confided in no idle gossip. I have adduced no testimony not of my own knowledge,
or from those who are authorized to speak to
the question at issue, and with reference thereto,
with my hand upon my heart, and my eye on
Heaven, I call this House, and (I speak with
reverence) I call my God to witness the truth
of all the assertions made from my own convictions and knowledge, and my entire confidence
in the credibility of all the testimony which I
have adduced from others.

Note.—The object of this speech being, not to defend
any doctrine of the Catholic Church, but simply to defend the Church and its members from the charge of
holding as an article of faith, what is not a part of the
Catholic creed, it has been deemed appropriate to copy
the following from a Prayer Book, in much use among
the Catholics:

"This [the Pope's] commission regards only the
Kingdom of Heaven, that is the society which Christ
established upon earth to be one fold under one shep-

herd, to be brought by the practice of virtue and the power of His institutions, through His merits to the possession of eternal glory. This commission extends not, then, a power to the Pope of interfering in the temporal, the civil, or the political regulations of nations." [15]

[15] The above note is appended to Mr. Chandler's speech, as here faithfully copied from the official Congressional publication.

Appendix.

❦❦❦

Joseph Ripley Chandler.

❦❦❦

JOSEPH RIPLEY CHANDLER, whose memorable oration on the Temporal Power of the Pope forms the present number of *Educational Briefs,* was born in Kingston, Plymouth County, Massachusetts, 25 August, 1792. After his marriage, in 1815, he settled in Philadelphia, where he died, 10 July, 1880. His life of sixty-five years in Philadelphia made him one of the most conspicuous and honorable public men in the history of the city during the nineteenth century.

He was a teacher and a principal of a successful school for eleven years; editor of *The United States Gazette,* and afterwards an editorial writer for one of the oldest of American newspapers, *The North American;* a member of the City Council (1832 to 1848); a member of Congress for three terms (1849 to 1855); the first President of the Board of Directors of Girard College; United States Minister at Naples (1858 to 1861); the representative, at the International Congress in London, 1872, of the Philadelphia Society for Alleviating the Miseries of Public Prisons; a member of the Convention for revis-

ing the Constitution of Pennsylvania (1836);
a citizen who took an active part in all leading
municipal affairs; a leader, and, to a great extent,
director of a powerful political party; a journal-
ist, diplomat, and philanthropist.

For the last twenty-one years of his life he
was a consistent, active, devout Catholic; interested in everything pertaining to the Church
and laboring for every measure which promoted
religion and morality. The press of the city of
Philadelphia, at his death, with singular unanim-
ity, told the story of his life in terms of unqual-
ified praise and commendation.

No better illustration can be found of a model
citizen, loyal and devoted to all that is highest
and best for his country's welfare and at the
same time a fervent, loyal and practical Catholic. Of his speech, which is here reproduced
from the official *Congressional Globe,* it has
been said:

"One of the most eloquent and impressive
speeches ever made upon the floor of the House
of Representatives Joseph R. Chandler delivered
in reply to the criticism made upon the Catholic
Church by the Hon. Nathaniel P. Banks of
Massachusetts. It is not often that set speeches
are listened to in that body, but Mr. Chandler's
commanded rapt attention from the first word
to the last, and, at the close, he was cordially
congratulated by his party adversaries, as well
as party friends, Mr. Banks himself being
among the number."

PRESIDENT ROOSEVELT'S LETTER ON RELIGION IN POLITICS.

"*Nov. 6, 1908.*

"*My Dear Sir:* I have received your letter, running in part as follows:

"'While it is claimed almost universally that religion should not enter into politics, yet there is no denying that it does, and the mass of the voters that are not Catholics will not support a man for any office, especially for President of the United States, who is a Roman Catholic.

"'Since Taft has been nominated for President by the Republican party it is being circulated and is constantly urged as a reason for not voting for Taft that he is an infidel (Unitarian) and wife and brother Roman Catholics. * * * If his feelings are in sympathy with the Roman Catholic Church on account of his wife and brother being Catholics, that would be objectionable to a sufficient number of voters to defeat him. On the other hand, if he is an infidel, that would be sure to mean defeat. * * * I am writing this letter for the sole purpose of giving Mr. Taft an opportunity to let the world know what his religious belief is.'

RECEIVED MANY QUERIES.

"I received many such letters as yours during the campaign, expressing dissatisfaction with Mr. Taft on religious grounds; some of them on the ground that he was a Unitarian, and others on the ground that he was suspected to be in sympathy with Catholics. I did not answer any of these letters during the campaign because I regarded it as an outrage even, to agitate such a question as a man's religious convictions, with the purpose of influencing a political election. But now that the campaign is over, when there is opportunity for men calmly to consider whither such propositions as those you make in your letter would lead, I wish to invite them to consider them, and I have selected your letter to answer because you advance both the objections commonly urged against Mr. Taft; namely, that he is a Unitarian and also that he is suspected of sympathy with the Catholics.

"You ask that Mr. Taft shall 'let the world know what his religious belief is.' This is purely his own private concern, and it is a matter between him and his Maker, a matter for his own conscience; and to require it to be made public under penalty of political discrimination is to negative the first principles of our Government, which guarantee complete religious liberty, and the right to each man to act in religious affairs as his own conscience dictates. Mr. Taft never asked my advice in the matter, but if he had asked it, I would have emphatically advised him against thus stating publicly his religious belief. The demand for a statement of a candidate's religious belief can have no meaning except that there may be discrimination for or against him because of that belief. Discrimination against the holder of one faith means retaliatory discrimination against men of other faiths. The inevitable result of entering upon such a practice would be an abandonment of our real freedom of conscience and a reversion to the dreadful conditions of religious dissension which in so many lands have proved fatal to true liberty, to true religion and to all advance in civilization.

"OUTRAGE AGAINST LIBERTY."

"To discriminate against a thoroughly upright citizen because he belongs to some particular Church, or because, like Abraham Lincoln, he has not avowed his allegiance to any Church, is an outrage against that liberty of conscience which is one of the foundations of American life. You are entitled to know whether a man seeking your suffrage is a man of clean and upright life, honorable in all his dealings with his fellows and fit by qualification and purpose to do well in the great office for which he is a candidate; but you are not entitled to know matters which lie purely between himself and his Maker. If it is proper or legitimate to oppose a man for being a Unitarian, as was John Quincy Adams, for instance; as is the Rev. Edward Everett Hale, at the present moment chaplain of the Senate, and an American of whose life all good Americans are proud, then it would be equally proper to support or oppose a man because of his view on justification by faith, or the method of administering the sacrament or the gospel of salvation by works. If you once enter on such a career there is absolutely no limit at which you can legitimately stop.

"So much for your objections to Mr. Taft because he is a Unitarian. Now, for your objections to him because you think his wife and brother to be Roman Catholics. As it happened they are not but if they were, or if Mr. Taft were a Roman Catholic himself, it ought not to effect in the slightest degree any man's supporting him for the position of President.

"FOULLY SLANDER COUNTRYMEN."

"You say that 'the mass of the voters that are not Catholics will not support a man for any office, especially for President of the United States, who is a Roman Catholic.' I believe that when you say this you foully slander your fellow-countrymen. I do not for one moment believe that the mass of our fellow citizens, or that any considerable number of our fellow citizens, can be influenced by such narrow bigotry as to refuse to vote for any thoroughly upright and fit man because he happens to have a particular religious creed. Such a consideration should never be treated as a reason for either supporting or opposing a candidate for a political office.

"Are you aware that there are several States in this Union where the majority of the people are now Catholics? I should reprobate in the severest terms the Catholics who in those States (or in any other States) refused to vote for the most fit man because he happened to be a Protestant, and my condemnation would be exactly as severe for a Protestant who under reversed circumstances refused to vote for a Catholic.

"In public life I am happy to say that I have known many men who were elected and constantly re-elected to office in districts where the great majority of their constituents were of a different religious belief. I know Catholics who have for many years represented constituencies mainly Protestant, and Protestants who have for many years represented constituencies mainly Catholic; and among the Congressmen whom I know particularly well was one man of Jewish faith who represented a district in which there were hardly any Jews at all. All of these men by their very existence in political life rebuke the slander you have uttered against your fellow Americans.

MANY CREEDS IN CABINET.

"I believe that this Republic will endure for many centuries. If so, there will doubtless be among its Presidents Protestants and Catholics and very probably at some time Jews. I have consistently tried while President to act in relation to my fellow Americans of Catholic faith as I hope that any future President who happens to be a Catholic will act toward his fellow Americans of Protestant faith. Had I followed any other course I should have felt that I was unfit to represent the American people.

"In my Cabinet at the present moment there sit side by side Catholic and Protestant, Christian and Jew, each man chosen because in my belief he is peculiarly fit to exercise on behalf of all our people the duties of the office to which I have appointed him. In no case does the man's religious belief in any way influence his discharge of his duties, save as it makes him more eager to act justly and uprightly in his relations to all men. The same principles that have obtained in appointing the members of my Cabinet, the highest officials under me, the officials to whom is intrusted the work of carrying out all the important policies of my administration, are the principles upon which all good Americans should act in choosing, whether by election or appointment, the men to fill any office from the highest to the lowest in the land.

        " Yours truly,

                " THEODORE ROOSEVELT.

" MR. J. C. MARTIN, *Dayton, Ohio.*"

LETTER TO PRESIDENT ROOSEVELT FROM THE NEW YORK CITY SYNODICAL CONFERENCE OF THE EVANGELICAL LUTHERAN CHURCH OF AMERICA:

" Convinced of your deep sincerity, and in full agreement with you as to the fundamental principle of the separation of Church and State as enunciated in your letter to Mr. J. C. Martin, members and pastors of our Church, and other Churches as well, have been amazed to see the indiscriminate and self-contradictory application you make of that principle itself, and this in the stricture made by you on those who might refuse to vote for a Roman Catholic for the highest office in the gift of our people.

" Of course, it is subversive of the basic principle of a real separation of Church and State to permit the religious belief or non-belief of any candidate for public office to determine the casting of one's vote for or against such candidates, except when that very religious belief or non-belief antagonizes this principle of complete separation of Church and State and all those rights and liberties which are included therein and safeguarded thereby. We agree with you, therefore, that those citizens are to be severely criticised who vote against a man merely because he is a Unitarian, a Jew, a Methodist or any other religionist.

" But are you not aware of the fact that the Roman Catholic Church has, again and again, for centuries

63

back and down to modern times, through its official head and other authorities, denounced as wholly wrong and as things to be tolerated only so long as they cannot be changed, the complete separation of Church and State, full religious liberty, freedom of conscience, of speech, of the press and that, moreover, it proclaims its teachings and principles to be unchangeable, and boasts of being ' semper idem.' . . .

"Even Cardinal Gibbons in his book *The Faith of Our Fathers* makes these significant statements, the best he has to offer in vindication of the Church against the charge that it is opposed to civil and religious liberty: 'A man enjoys religious liberty when he possesses the free right of worshiping God according to the dictates of a right conscience and of practising the form of religion most in accordance with his duties to God.'

"I shall quote the great theologian Becanus, who taught the doctrine of the schools of Catholic theology at the time when the struggle was strongest between Catholicity and Protestantism. He says that religious liberty may be tolerated by a ruler when it would do more harm to the State or to the Community to repress it. The ruler may even enter into a contract in order to secure to his subjects this freedom in religious matters, and when once a contract is made, it must be observed absolutely in every point, just as every other lawful and honest contract.

"What else are these obviously mildest declarations of Romanists but a confirmation of the charge that the Roman Catholic Church does not stand for full and perfect religious liberty as understood by all Americans and defined in our federal Constitution, that every man shall be free, not only to worship God according to the dictates of a 'right conscience and to practise a religion most in accordance with his duties to God,' but according to his conscience and his conception of his duties to God, right or wrong, so long as he is not thereby led to endanger the Equal rights

64

and liberties of his neighbor or to interfere with the free exercise of the government's power in the Equal protection of all citizens?

"Are we not then compelled to maintain that a loyal Roman Catholic who fully understands the allegiance required of him by the Pope can never sincerely subscribe to the federal constitution, or, if he does subscribe to it, never can be expected to abide by it, enforce and defend it?

" Papacy and Vaticanism cannot be separated from the Roman Catholic religion. If any one should entertain an idea that this were possible, let him read Cardinal Gibbons's book.

" How then could we, as firm believers in the principle of complete separation of Church and State, and the liberties based thereon and safeguarded thereby, conscientiously and consistently help to elect to the Presidency a member of the Roman Catholic Church so long as that Church does not officially, through its pontiff or church council, revoke its diametrically opposed declarations?

"Are the two millions and more Lutherans of this country, not to speak of the millions of other Protestants who take this position for the reasons stated, to be accused of bigotry or fanaticism because of their stand, aye, be denounced as being disloyal American citizens?

" We protest that it is neither personal feeling nor religious antagonism which determines our attitude in this matter, but solely our disagreement with the Roman Catholic Church on this basic principle, a disagreement growing out of the rejection and denunciation by the Roman Catholic Church of that very principle which you admonish all faithfully to uphold, not only in theory, but in practice.

" We do not wish to be understood as though to accuse the bulk of the Roman Catholics of being disloyal citizens. We sincerely believe a great many do not fully realize that the position the hierarchy of

65

their church maintains, with reference to the principle in question, especially in view of the outgivings
of their teachers in this country, and that, if it came
to an issue compelling a decision either for the
Constitution or the papal hierarchy they would decide
in favor of the former, upholding the Constitution of
the United States. Yet, in determining our attitude in
this matter, especially when it comes to electing a man
to the highest public office, we must be guided by
the official teachings of the recognized authorities of
the Roman Catholic Church.

"We have considered it to be our duty not to keep
silence in this matter, because, in our judgment, that
would have been an act of cowardice, nor do we wish
to do any one an injustice, nor in any manner traduce
any man or body of men.

INVITE REPLY FROM PRESIDENT.

"If, therefore, in aught we have said we are laboring under error, we shall be pleased to have you en-
lighten us, and with us the millions who occupy the
same position, and shall be sincerely grateful to you
for such enlightenment. But, if we are right in our
contention and position, we ask you to show your un-
questioned sincerity and courage by an acknowledgment of the correctness of our contention and the
attitude based thereon."

The letter was signed by Rev. William Schoenfeld,
pastor of Emmanuel Church, and Rev. Martin Walker,
pastor of St. Matthew's Church, the members of the
Conference Committee.

LETTER OF THE LUTHERAN PASTORAL AS-
SOCIATION AND THE GERMAN LUTHERAN
PASTORAL CONFERENCE OF PHILADEL-
PHIA TO PRESIDENT ROOSEVELT.

"The Hon. Theodore Roosevelt, President of the
United States, Washington, D. C.

"*Dear Sir:* The undersigned beg leave to inform you
that the English Pastoral Association and the German
Pastoral Conference, belonging to the General Council of the Evangelical Lutheran Church in North
America—the second largest Lutheran body in this
country—at their regular sessions, held November 16,
have unanimously indorsed the published protest of the
Lutheran pastors in New York against certain statements made in your letter to Mr. J. C. Martin,
Dayton, O., as reported in the daily press.

"We feel constrained to join this protest in the interest of 'that liberty of conscience which is one of the
foundations of American life.' We stand firmly by our
Constitution, 'that no religious test shall ever be required as a qualification to any office or public trust
under the United States.' We look upon the declaration that Congress shall make no law respecting an es-
tablishment of religion, or prohibiting the free exercise thereof' as the magna charta of religious freedom
in these United States.

"We do not presume to judge any of our fellow
citizens on account of the religious beliefs which they
may conscientiously hold. Where there is nothing in
the religious tenets of any of our fellow citizens that
antagonizes those precious principles of religious freedom and of the separation of Church and State, we
have to consider a man's religion entirely as his own
private affair between himself and his God, and when
it comes to the question of voting for such a man as
the President of the United States we have only to
ask if he is 'a man of clean and upright life, honorable in all his dealings with his fellows and fit by

qualification and purpose to do well in the great office for which he is a candidate.'

"We would recognize this standard even when the candidate would differ from us in matters of faith as widely as the Jew or the Unitarian. But, unfortunately, the case is different when the candidate is a loyal and devoted member of the Roman Catholic Church. And, in this case, it is this Church with which we have to do and the principles for which she stands in regard to the relation of Church and State, freedom of conscience and worship. We are not at a loss to know the exact spirit of the Church of Rome and her principles on those important points. They have been declared and reiterated by the recognized rulers of that Church, the Bishops of Rome, in language which admits of no possible misunderstanding or misinterpretation.

POPE BONIFACE'S BULL.

"The famous Bull 'Unam Sanctam' of Pope Boniface VIII, A. D. 1302, distinctly claims that all power, both secular and spiritual, is given to the Church. (Uterque gladius in potestate ecclesiae, spiritualis et materialis.) That the temporal power (of the State) must be subject to the spiritual power of the Church. (Temporalem autoritatem spirituali subjici potestati.) It is laid down as an absolute condition of salvation for every human creature that it must be subject to the Roman Pontiff (Subesse Romano Pontifici omni humanae creaturae declaramus, dicimus, definimus et pronuntiamus omnino .esse de necessitate salutis), this submission including secular affairs as well as spiritual.

"In his Encyclical Letter of August 15, 1854, Pope Pius IX declares: 'The absurd and erroneous doctrines or ravings in defense of liberty of conscience are a most pestilential error—a pest of all others most to be dreaded in a State.'

"The same ruler of the Roman Catholic Church,

68

in his Encyclical of December 8, 1864, condemns those who hold that 'the State should have no power to inflict certain fixed penalties on those who offend against the Catholic religion.' He also condemns those who hold 'that liberty of conscience is the inherent right of every man.'

"Also those who hold 'that any citizen has the right to express publicly by speech or print whatever he thinks, and that neither ecclesiastical nor secular authorities should have the right to limit such liberty.

."This Encyclical of December, 1864, culminates in a syllabus which, among 80 different statements or opinions, condemns the following:

"No. 15. 'Every man is at liberty to accept that religion which, in the light of his reason, seems to him the true one.' Condemned by the syllabus.

"No. 24. 'That the Church has no secular power, directly or indirectly, and that she ought not to employ force.' Condemned by the syllabus.

"No. 45. 'That to the State belongs the supervision and direction of the public schools.' Condemned by the syllabus.

"No. 55. 'That the Church is to be separate from the State and the State separate from the Church.' Condemned by the syllabus.

"No. 77. 'That it was no longer required in our times that the Catholic religion should be maintained as the only State religion, to the exclusion of all other cults.' Condemned by the syllabus.

DECLARATIONS OPPOSED.

"Such are the official declarations of the Church of Rome, affirmed and reaffirmed by its mouthpiece, the Bishop of Rome, the principles which every loyal and devout Roman Catholic is bound to believe, hold and enforce under penalty of losing his soul—due allowance, of course, being made for the suspension of their actual enforcement at certain times and places when it would be inexpedient or impossible. (Temporum ratione habita.)

"It is the attitude of the Church of Rome, so clearly antagonistic to our American convictions and the Constitution of the United States, that makes it so difficult, yea, impossible, for us as patriotic citizens to vote for a Roman Catholic as President, if such a case should arise. The difficulty is caused not by 'narrow bigotry' on our part, but by the presumptions of the Church of Rome, which time and again have proved so disastrous to the peace and prosperity of nations.

"The difficulty could be removed if the Roman authorities would be ready and willing to reconsider and cancel these declarations of principles which are so essentially antagonistic to our American Constitution, liberty of conscience and the separation of Church and State.

"These official Roman Catholic declarations on the relation between Church and State, religious liberty, etc., impress us—and we hope will continue to impress the majority of loyal American citizens and voters —as representing that very outrage which you, Mr. President, so justly and severely condemn, 'an outrage against the liberty of conscience, which is one of the foundations of American life.'

"We appeal to your well-known sense of fairness and manliness that, instead of denouncing our position on this great life question of our country as 'narrow bigotry,' you will rather recognize the conscientious patriotism which prompts our action. It is our earnest hope that you, as the President of this glorious republic, will always be the most fearless champion of liberty of conscience, religion and worship, realizing the true dangers by which our country is beset and defending it against the principles mentioned above which threaten the very foundations of our American life.

"We respectfully submit these statements for your earnest and candid consideration, invoking God's richest blessings upon you, our beloved and honored President.

"In behalf of the Lutheran Pastoral Association and the German Lutheran Pastoral Conference of Philadelphia, Pa.

" A. SPAETH,

" JACOB FRY,

" LUTHER D. REED,

" E. J. HEILMAN,

"*Joint Committee.*

Lutheran Theological Seminary, Mt. Airy, Philadelphia, November 18, 1908.

RESOLUTIONS OF THE PHILADELPHIA CONFERENCE OF BAPTIST MINISTERS.

"In view of a recently published letter from the President of the United States and of the public interest in the matter in question:

"The Philadelphia Conference of Baptist Ministers thinks it well to make the following statement of principles and convictions:

"(1) We are heartily in accord with the Chief Magistrate as to the absolute separation of Church and State, the perfect freedom of conscience, the distinction between the spiritual and secular spheres and the impropriety of religious tests for civil office imposed by law; principles long maintained by Baptists. We believe that Americans in choosing their rulers and representatives should consider ability, fitness, integrity and correct political principles rather than religious belief. And we should deplore the infusion into politics of sectarian strife and bitterness.

"(2) At the same time we cannot shut our eyes to the fact that if these principles are to be successfully and honorably carried out they must be carried out by men who believe in them and not by men who do not understand them or are hostile to them.

71

"(3) The Roman Catholic Church claims infallibility, centred in the Pope when he speaks *ex cathedra*. This necessarily involves his right to define the sphere of his own authority. In his so-called infallible teaching the Pope has condemned the separation of the Church and the State as a matter of right, the legal equality of all sects, the unrestricted circulation of the Bible, liberty of conscience, and freedom of thought and investigation. Every true Catholic is bound by his profession of faith to accept these teachings. When Catholics favor religious freedom, and the separation of Church and State, in this country it is avowedly or tacitly as a matter of necessity or expediency. Thus is secured to them the largest liberty. But should they ever attain an overwhelming majority, their own statements show that they might feel in duty bound to carry out, as far as possible, not American ideas of civil and religious liberty, but the teachings of the Pope. Moreover, the Pope stubbornly maintains his claims to the temporal power, as against the kingdom of Italy; he desires to be recognized as a great power in the earth by the nations, and as such to have diplomatic relations with them. The Church of Rome is hostile to our system of non-sectarian public schools, and demands a portion of the public money to support its parochial schools. Furthermore, history shows that Rome has approved of persecution for the suppression of heresy; and the doctrine of Papal infallibility would seem to preclude the idea of retraction of dogma or decree.

"(4) Recognizing, therefore, that the Roman Catholic Church is not merely a religious organization, but an astute and persistent claimant of political influence, and the foe, on principle, of the American idea of civil and religious liberty, we assert that American citizens may be justified in declining to vote for Roman Catholics for high office, in the State, at least, until the Romish Church shall officially and frankly change its attitude. The same principle applies to the adherents of the Morman hierarchy or in any similar case.

72

"(5) We respect the high office of the President of the United States, but we dissent most earnestly from the statement that it is bigotry for an American citizen to refuse his vote to a candidate bound to support the policies of the Romish Church; and just as we disapprove of legal disabilities and tests on the ground of religious beliefs, so equally and strenuously we maintain the inalienable right of every voter to cast his ballot according to the dictates of his own conscience and judgment, uncontrolled by any ecclesiastical power or deliverance, Roman Catholic or any other, and without reproach or obloquy.

"(6) We regard the attitude of the high officials of the Roman Catholic Church toward both our school system and our separation of Church and State as unwise for the best interests of their own membership and hostile and disloyal to the country, and we appeal to the great mass of our Roman Catholic fellow citizens whose intelligent loyalty we do not desire to question, to assert their right to think and act in harmony with the governmental idea of their own country, instead of the un-American ideas of the old countries. We remind them that our Government has already given them greater religious liberty than any Government where Church and State are united. We urge them to stand by the free public schools, that bulwark of our liberties, which a generous Government provides for them, and to help us maintain the perpetual separation of Church and State."

LETTER OF THE REV. MR. LARSON TO MR. WILLIAM H. TAFT, REPUBLICAN CANDIDATE FOR PRESIDENT OF THE UNITED STATES, WITH MR. TAFT'S REPLY.

"*Dear Sir:* Pardon a few questions from an humble St. Paul preacher. I wish, however, first of all to state that I have been an admirer of President Roosevelt, and have considered him in many respects an ideal President. Notwithstanding this, it seems to me that he has put you in an embarrassing position, when taking upon himself to be your protector and telling the people of this country what you are and what you will be.

"The questions I wish to ask concern your work in the Philippine Islands and your attitude toward the Catholic Church. Was it upon your recommendation that $7,000,000 were paid to the Catholic Church out of the United States Treasury, and that the Pope was consulted regarding this deal? Did such a deal voice the sentiment of the Filipinos? Was the uprising in the Philippines mostly in the Spanish Government or against the Catholic friars?

"In a speech in New York some time ago you made a plea for the Catholic Church in the Philippines, making the statement that the Church was very poor. Is it not true that half the population, or 3,000,000 people, are not Catholics?

"I understand that the present Governor is a Catholic? Are you aware of the attitude he is taking against Protestants, especially the teachers of the public schools, who are forbidden to take any interest in any Protestant work, such as teaching in Sunday-school or taking part in religious services?

"Have not thousands of dollars been paid to friars for libraries they have claimed to have been burned? Is it not your conviction and policy that Catholic dignitaries and the Catholic Church should have greater consideration from a public official, and especially from the Chief Executive of our nation, than any other recognized religious body?

"The questions are asked in all sincerity with a view to get just and right in my political attitude. I have not one word to say against the Catholic Church or any other denomination, but I do contend that the one shall not have any more favors than the other.

"Although I am at present confined to the hospital, I have decided to use my influence, both with voice

74

and pen, in favor of the man who is ready and willing to uphold, protect and promulgate the true spirit of our Constitution, and religious, as well as commercial, industrial and social orders. The Swedish Americans are not so great in number, but they are loyal citizens, and I am quite sure they will be heard from in the coming national election."

"This letter is not written for the purpose of making you believe that the writer is a person who has some wonderful influence or one that would be a great vote getter for any political party. This is simply a personal letter—I have no objection to making it public —and if you choose to answer, well and good; if not, I take it for granted that you do not care to go on record concerning the question, and in any event I am answered.

"I am not a politician, but I am intensely interested in the welfare of our country, and shall lend all the influence and power that I have to see men elected to office who shall feel the responsibility of the confidence placed in them by a sovereign people.

"With greatest respect I am, very truly yours,
"MAGNUS LARSON,
"Pastor of the Swedish Baptist Church, St. Paul, Minn."

JUDGE TAFT'S ANSWER.

"*My Dear Sir:* I have your letter of September 26. You ask me whether $7,000,000 were paid to the Catholic Church out of the United States Treasury on my recommendation. I reply that it was not. The friars' agricultural lands in the Philippines — 425,000 acres, or about that amount—were purchased from the corporation formed by the three orders of the friars in the Philippines, and the money was paid from bonds issued by the Philippine Government under the authority of Congress, and is a charge upon the Philippine Islands. The purchase was approved by the Filipinos.

"The uprising in the Philippines was against the

75

Spanish Government, and the Spanish friars whom the Government used as policemen in attempting to stamp out the sedition and political discussion among the Filipinos.

"In a speech in New York I did not make a plea for the Roman Catholic Church in the Philippines, except to say this:

"That the influence of all the churches in the Philippines was necessary for the uplifting of the people, and that therefore every one would desire the prosperity of all the churches, and that as the Roman Catholic Church had the largest following every one, Protestants or Catholics, would desire its prosperity; that it was in a deplorable condition due to the change in the situation, in which the Government paid its expenses, to one in which it was bound to look to its parishioners for support, and that they were in the habit of deriving benefit from the Church and not contributing to it. It made a difficult situation for the Roman Church.

"It is not true that half of the population, or 3,000,000 of the people, are not Roman Catholics. There was at one time a large defection, due to the so-called Aglipay schism, but it has not been maintained in number and many are returning to the Roman Catholic Church, while others are going into Protestant churches.

"The present Governor is a Roman Catholic, but he is one of the most careful men in maintaining an impartial attitude between Catholics and Protestants that we could possibly have. He does not forbid teachers to take an interest in Protestant Sunday-school work or to attend Protestant churches. Only by law there is enjoined upon teachers the non-teaching of religious matters in public schools.

"No money has been paid to the friars for libraries that they claim to have been burned, so far as I can recollect. The sum of money paid was for rent and damage to convents or rectories by United States soldiers.

"I do not think that Catholic dignitaries in the Catholic churches should have greater consideration from a public official than any other regularly organized religious body. It has happened that by reason of the fact that the Philippine Government under Spain was inextricably united with the Catholic Church, and that that union had to be severed and property and other interests had to be assigned to the Church or to the State, I had much to do with the hierarchy of the Catholic Church and visited Rome in order to bring about a settlement. The settlement has been brought about, and, in my judgment, it is fair and just to all parties.

"I am not a Catholic and have not been affiliated with the Catholic Church. All I have attempted to do was to do justice to that Church and to the Filipino people. I have treated that church exactly as I would have treated any other church had it been in a similar position to that of the Catholic Church.

"I may add, with respect to the friars' lands, that the purchase was a political and agrarian one rather than a commercial one. There were 60,000 tenants on the friars' lands who, because of the confiscatory measure passed by the so-called Malolos Aguinaldo convention, refused to recognize the title of the friars.

"This title was as good a title as there was in the Philippines, and it authorized the friars to go into our courts, when they were established, and institute 60,000 eviction suits. This would have led to a second revolution, and it was an absolute political necessity that we should buy the lands and then attempt to dispose of them, as we are now doing, to the tenants on long and even terms of purchase.

"Very sincerely yours,

"WILLIAM H. TAFT."

"The Rev. Magnus Larson, First Swedish Baptist Church, 361 Sims street, St. Paul, Minn."

CARDINAL MANNING ON THE CIVIL ALLE-GIANCE OF CATHOLICS.

Mr. Gladstone, in his "Expostulation" with the Catholics of the British Empire on the decrees of the Vatican Council, wrote as follows:

"England is entitled to ask and to know in what way the obedience required by the Pope and Council of the Vatican is to be reconciled with the integrity of Civil Allegiance?"

His Eminence Cardinal Manning, the Archbishop of Westminster, answered at once the following letter [1] in the London *Times*:

ARCHBISHOP'S HOUSE, WESTMINSTER,
November 7, 1874.

TO THE EDITOR OF THE TIMES,

Sir: The gravity of the subject on which I address you, affecting as it must, every Catholic in the British Empire, will, I hope, obtain from your courtesy the publication of this letter.

This morning I received a copy of a pamphlet entitled *The Vatican Decrees in their Bearing on Civil Allegiance.* I find in it a direct appeal to myself, both for the office I hold and for the writings I have published. I gladly acknowledge the duty that lies upon me for both these reasons. I am bound by the office I bear not to suffer a day to pass without repelling from the Catholics of this country the lighest imputation upon their loyalty; and, for my teaching, I am ready to show that the principles I have ever taught are beyond impeachment upon that score.

It is true, that in page 57 of the pamphlet Mr. Gladstone expresses his belief "that many of his Roman Catholic friends and fellow countrymen are, to say the least of it, as good citizens as himself." But as the whole pamphlet is an elaborate argument to prove that the teaching of the Vatican Council renders it im-

[1] Purcell's *Life of Cardinal Manning*, Vol. II, p. 473.

possible for them to be so, I cannot accept this grateful acknowledgment, which implies that they are good citizens because they are at variance with the Catholic Church.

I should be wanting in duty to the Catholics of this country and to myself if I did not give a prompt contradiction to this statement, and if I did not with equal promptness affirm that the loyalty of our civil allegiance is, not in spite of the teaching of the Catholic Church, but because of it.

The sum of the argument in the pamphlet just published to the world is this: That by the Vatican decrees such a change has been made in the relations of Catholics to the Civil Power of States, that it is no longer possible for them to render the same undivided Civil Allegiance as it was possible for Catholics to render before the promulgation of those Decrees.

In answer to this it is for the present sufficient to affirm:

I. That the Vatican Decrees have in no jot or tittle changed either the obligations or the conditions of Civil Allegiance.

II. That the Civil Allegiance of Catholics is as undivided as that of all Christians, and of all who recognize a divine or natural moral law.

III. That the Civil Allegiance of no man is unlimited; and therefore the Civil Allegiance of all men who believe in God, or are governed by conscience, is in that sense divided.

IV. In this sense, and in no other, can it be said with truth that the Civil Allegiance of Catholics is divided. The Civil Allegiance of every Christian man in England is limited by conscience and the Law of God; and the Civil Allegiance of Catholics is limited neither less nor more.

The public peace of the British Empire has been consolidated in the last half century by the Elimination of religious conflicts and inequalities from our laws. . . .

The author of the pamphlet, in his first line, assures us that his "purpose is not polemical but pacific." I am sorry that so good an intention should have so widely erred in the selection of the means.

But my purpose is neither to criticise nor to controvert. My desire and my duty, as an Englishman, as a Catholic, and as a pastor, is to claim for my flock and for myself a Civil Allegiance as pure, as true, and as loyal as is rendered by the distinguished author of the pamphlet, or by any subject of the British Empire.

Your obedient servant,
H. E. MANNING.

CPSIA information can be obtained
at www.ICGtesting.com
Printed in the USA
BVHW04*1220210918

528171BV00010B/460/P

9 780484 579599